Helpful Tips For Any Type of Business

Authored by Christi Hubbard

Patriotic & Family Oriented Business owner
CFC 19270

Dedication:

I need to give thanks to my Mom, Janet Hubbard Shreve for always believing in me. Also to God above for always guiding me true and straight.

I give thanks to my wonderful and steadfast friends and business associates who always give wonderful suggestions. "You know so much you should be a consultant and charge for your knowledge." "You should write a book."

I give thanks to my sons, Matthew and Mark Myers for helping me out with my company clients while I took the time to jump right in and write the book inside a month.

Thank you to Melissa Vazquez, an author in her own right, for sharing CreateSpace with me so I could easily write and self-publish the book.

ISBN-13: 978-1500129293
ISBN-10: 1500129291

Table of Contents:

Introduction

A little background. I own and operate 3 companies all with one goal in mind, to help others in need. I will be writing about my personal and professional experiences while still keeping my clients confidential. If by educating and speaking about what I've encountered helps just 1 person, it will be worth it.

Animal Rescue & Veteran Support Services, Corp (Veteran Rescue ®) is a *501c3 nonprofit* created by **Ms. Christi Hubbard** (primary owner, founder and CFO) to use animal assisted therapy to assist Veterans in their rehabilitation and reorientation through various services. Since 2011 we have been assisting veterans with home repair projects, rehabilitating rescued animals and paring them together to heal both with plenty of care. http://veteranrescue.org/ We have won 2 awards to date. Veteran Rescue ® is a registered trademark of Animal Rescue & Veteran Support Services, Corp. christi@veteranrescue.org "A Warrior's Sanctuary"

100% tax deductible receipts. #VeteranRescue #taxdeductible #animalshelter #dog #cat #donate #veteran #PTSD #retreat #horse #therapy

Wildcat's Sanctuary and Ranch Corp is called upon to handle all kinds of questions, pets, and furry children. You can see them as we walk them, play with them, introduce them to others, and in some cases steer clear of them so mom doesn't abandon them.

Summer means pet sitters are in high demand. Schedule your sitter today and know peace of mind. christi@wildcatsanctuaryranch.com

We have won 4 awards to date. http://www.wildcatsanctuaryranch.com/

We are experienced in all manner of breeds. We are licensed and insured. We have been voted the best in Lake Mary 4 years in a row. We use lots of love and treats. No harsh choker collars, no shock collars, no expensive courses. We work right in our home and neighborhood. We offer multiple discounts and accept credit card payments. "Ask for the Best, Ask for Wildcat!

Welcome to Home For Heroes ®

Home For Heroes ® **Ms. Christi Hubbard** (primary owner) to use PTSD videos and Reality TV in showcasing Veterans healing on the ranch. A percentage of all proceeds are donated to Veteran Rescue ®.

Home For Heroes ® is a registered trademark of Home For Heroes Productions, LLC. "United We Stand, Divided We Fail."

To contact for more information, interest in investing or being filmed please email info@homeforheroestv.com
http://www.homeforheroestv.com/

Amazon smile. Thank you for shopping!
http://smile.amazon.com/ch/32-0337515

Ms. Hubbard was raised on a small ten acre farm in the woods of Brooksville, Florida, with lots of animals. She's actively cared for a variety of pets since she was a small child. These early experiences impacted her in a profound way. Later, she noticed a distinct lack of animal care in her area when owners traveled on vacation. The owners often boarded their pets with a vet, typically in cages. Wildcat asked, "Who wants to stay in a cage all day?" The answer – No one!

She has handled horses, rabbits, ferrets, cats, dogs, birds, hamsters and gerbils. Years ago, Christi discovered an ability to catch and hold any animal whether feral or domestic, regardless of bites and claws. She's also hand raised animal babies that were abandoned, sick or just taken too soon from their mother to ensure their health and well-being. Her love of animals is partially the reason she earned the moniker "Wildcat". She also showed the tenacity of a wild cat in her fighting techniques during her police academy training, so "Wildcat" was a natural fit.

Throughout her adult life, Ms. Hubbard has gained a lot of different understanding through a lot of diverse work experiences. Ms. Hubbard has worked in Law Enforcement, and has two associates degree, one in Law Enforcement and the other in Criminology. She has earned multiple certificates and gathered a long line of military connections, which include her dad, a Marine, her nephew in the Air Force, a cousin and brother in law both in the Army. A father in law also retired from the Navy. Wildcat Hubbard worked for three years for the local Sheriff's office. For fifteen years, she worked as a receptionist, then two years as a teller. After that, she spent five years in security. She's also done house and pet sitting and volunteering.

#ChristiHubbard #Wildcat

Getting started: Which Is Right For You

For Profit: INC, Corp, LLC or Non Profit/Not For Profit 501c3

Costs Involved of Each as of this writing: Varies By State

For Instance Florida: Provided By Sunbiz.org

Corporation Fees
PROFIT AND NON-PROFIT

Filing Fees	$ 35.00
Registered Agent Designation	$ 35.00
*Certified Copy (optional)	$ 8.75
TOTAL	$ 78.75

Limited Liability Company Fees
Annual Report (& Supplemental Fee) $ 138.75

Colorado **Courtesy Of:**
http://www.sos.state.co.us/pubs/info_center/fees/business.html

Profit corporations	Online fee
Articles of Incorporation	$50.00

Nonprofit corporations	Online fee

Articles of Incorporation	$50.00

Limited liability company	Online fee
Articles of Organization	$50.00

Kentucky Courtesy Of: http://www.sos.ky.gov/bus/business-filings/Pages/Fees.aspx

Domestic Corporations (Profit and Professional Service)

- Articles of Incorporation: $40.00 (pursuant to KRS 136.060, profit entities must add organization tax based on number of shares)

Domestic Corporations (Non-Profit)

- Articles of Incorporation: $8.00

Domestic Limited Liabliity Company (Profit, Non-Profit or Professional Service)

- Articles of Organization: $40.00

Virginia Courtesy Of: http://www.scc.virginia.gov/clk/formfee.aspx

Virginia Stock Corporations

The number of the form relates to the applicable statute in Title 13.1 of the Code of Virginia. All fee payments should be made payable to the State Corporation Commission.

SCC FORM #/FORMAT	FORM TITLE
Notice-DOC Notice-PDF	**Notice to Virginia Corporations**
Charter/Entrance-DOC Charter/Entrance-PDF	**Corporation Charter/Entrance Fee Schedule**

Washington DC Courtesy Of:
http://dcra.dc.gov/service/register-domestic-entity

General Corporate Filing - All Entities

Corporations Division Fees - General Corporate Filing - All Entities

Entity Type	Fee Description	Fee Amount
All Domestic & Foreign Filing Entities	Expedited same-day service	$100.00
All Domestic & Foreign Filing Entities	Expedited three day service	$50.00

Division Fees - Nonprofit Corporation

Corporations Division Fees - Nonprofit Corporation

Entity Type	Fee Description	Fee Amount
Domestic Nonprofit Corporation	Articles of incorporation	$80.00

Corporations Division Fees - Limited Liability Company

Corporations Division Fees - Limited Liability Company

Entity Type	Fee Description	Fee Amount
Domestic Limited Liability Company	Certificate of organization	$220.00

Washington Courtesy Of:
https://www.sos.wa.gov/corps/FEESCHEDULEEXPEDITEDSERVICE.aspx

Limited Liability Companies (Title 25.15 RCW)

Original Filings $180

Profit Corporations (Title 23B RCW)

Original Filings $180

Non-profit Corporations (Title 24.03 RCW)

Original Filings $ 30

Limited Liability Partnerships (Title 25.05 RCW)

Application for Registration $180

Texas Courtesy Of: https://direct.sos.state.tx.us/help/help-corp.asp?pg=fee

Information Requests, Copies & Certificates   Fee

Certificate of Fact (including Certificate of Existence or Status)
    $15

Long Form Certificate of Existence (Status plus list of filings)
    $25

As you can see pricing varies widely based on location and type of company being created.

Partnerships, Collaborations and Promises

As a business owner you always look to enriching and opening up your network to utilize collaborations or partners. In doing so you are looking at that person's track record, reputation, services offered, and how they sync with your own before making the initial approach.

I myself have made some bad collaboration choices and some good ones. I will tell you what mistakes I made and how to avoid them.

Bad choice #1: Take someone's word as gospel truth just because they say they are a military Veteran.

How to avoid this: Check around. See what connections you have in common and ask for referral or how long they've known. Check to see if they are a Veteran. They should be able to provide you with a copy of DD-214, if not you can check via a person you know is a Veteran. They access to resources a civilian does not. Google them, what are others saying about them?

Bad Choice #2: Collaborative Partnership, get all legal documents signed first. I actually have 2 documents still outstanding to be signed and returned from 2 legit Veteran owned companies we have recently collaborated with. We actually had our business name stolen by someone in Oregon. FAR put that stolen and fraudulent info on our SAM record.

How to avoid this: Be a pest. Get those documents signed. Be apologetic but sincere, and don't communicate further with details they need until those papers are signed.

Bad Choice #3: Services offered: We look to see that the service you offer meshes with ours. But sometimes you have a service we need, you offer a really good deal for us. We accept and suddenly your promises are no good. Communication goes out the door.

How to avoid this: Find a company with a brick and mortar building, go to them, get everything in writing. I can't harp on the importance of this enough. We all want to help our local start ups. We all want to support our Veteran entrepreneurs. We don't want to be taken advantage of.

Experience we always tell the tale. Do your homework, get collaborative Partnership details written down into an MOU legally binding or an attorney to write up a true partnership document spelling out everything. Have confidential agreements ready to be signed. Get referrals and search well before agreeing to anything. If you have a Board of Directors get them involved. It's a part of their job to help you weed out those just talking smack. Always verify what you were told. In the end you'll be glad you did.

K.I.S.S. Method

I first learned about the K.I.S.S. Method (Keep It Simple Stupid) while attending the police academy. I have discovered this is what agencies want in their reports, whether that agency is police, security, bank, etc. Giving too much information does not help them make informed decisions.

When this method should not be utilized is when Fundraising, building collaboration M.O.U. documents, partnership mergers, last will and testament, staff instructions, etc. Although staff instructions should have details it should be precise not K.I.S.S.

Fundraising tips that help everyone out. The trick to a successful campaign is for everyone to share it, not just 1 person. Everyone who shares it, also likes it, and invites people to it if it's an event. You put out all the details so there's very little to question, you give it plenty of time, share, share, share. You don't know how often your post is being seen by others. I also have a list of organizations that nonprofits should utilize to really get their feet operational without breaking the budget.

If your organization has a 501c3 letter, please create your accounts: IT'S FREE!

Here are some logins we have for places you can get software, donations really cheap or even free. I'll leave off government logins as you probably won't be going after government contracts. If you decide you do want that I can walk you through SAM, Cage, DUNS, and NAICS. We can also team up on government contracts as women owned businesses there are certain set asides held specifically for us and are over $1 million a year.

SBA offers 8a certifications which open up a lot of state and federal donations of supplies FYI.
https://eweb.sba.gov/gls/dsp_login.cfm?CFID=10958620&CFTOKE
N=3ae26b3d44984541-9955A6C7-CF5E-0B66-
696D026F2B0511BF&jsessionid=5e30caf362087ed5537f7f305241

2548164f

We have Grantstation for a year we received for $99 via Techsoup. Every Foundation, individual, and others who give grant money to 501c3 nonprofits. http://grantstation.com/

http://techsoup.org/ is an excellent resource for software. For instance we have Office 2013 suite for just $30. We received QuickBooks there too, again very cheap and affordable for those on a shoestring budget.

CFC (combined Federation Campaign) biggest source of funding per year. Again takes a 501c3 certification. 1 county in Florida donated $10,000.00 to us this year. Next year we already have 4 states approved including Kentucky. The downside here is the funds are paid quarterly and fees apply. I'm told big changes are coming for FY 2014.

Good360 http://good360.com/

Guidestar.org rates nonprofits and accepts donations for them.

Amazon Smile: http://smile.amazon.com/

Only 1 Agency wants specialized 501c3 to apply with state licensing to back them or SBA 8A certification. Fleet and Federal Surplus Property.

Also special note: the US Government holds auctions where you bid on pallets of items you need. This is a useful way to obtain start up needs.

M.O.U. Agreements and Partner Mergers of companies should be very detailed as they are a legal document. you want to let the other organization or company know exactly where each party stands in relation to starting out, active executive directives, operational line of command, if something were to go south, etc.

Last will and testament should be precise because you want people to know you have one and you want them to obey it. It's your life and death we're talking about here. So be clear. K.I.S.S. while detailed is the way to go, because you don't want to confuse the executor.

You would think by giving more information you would be imparting more data for the person to make an informed decision in reality you just confused the poor person.

#fundraising #notforprofits #nonprofits #taxdeductible #MOU

Service Dog or Pet

How to tell the difference between a Service Dog and a Pet with a Vest. Keep in mind there is also a Therapy Pet. So to classify in order of health related benefits and training:

Service Dog: The most strenuous training. Final test is videotaped. Most Service Dogs are raised from a litter that had specific Breeding criteria. Some are rescued and then trained. Vest or ID tags identifying as a Service Dog is not required by law but definitely immediately identifies you as one. If a person has a Service dog by law you cannot ask what is wrong with them or why they need one. You cannot deny them entrance anywhere. A Service Dog performs a specific task required to help the person who is the handler. The pair train together.

Therapy Dog/Pet: Therapy pets, I say pets because any pet can be a therapy providing services but not fully trained. Have training but for one reason or another does not qualify for Service. Cannot go anywhere with the person. Cannot wear a vest that says Service Dog or Service in Training.

Pet: Obedience trained but out in public displays aggression, bad behavior, does not immediately obey commands.

Always check to make sure you are dealing with a reputable agency or organization when it comes to picking a service dog.

"Get tired of seeing individuals claim a service pet that has a vest but fits in a handbag or a small carrier. Seeing them come into a grocery store or a restaurant, or church! Bit much and seems that many do it for attention. How can a dog the size of a rat when it is wet be called a service animal?"

There are widely debated pros/cons of any type of dog being used for a Service Dog. What is important is the bond created, the training, and passing of a videotaped test proving the dog in question can perform the needed services and functions for the human.

Working with Animals

I have been working with animals since childhood. Each represents its own unique challenges.

Horses: Bite, Kick, Rear, Colic, Go riding, Buck you off

Dogs: Feral or Tame: Bite, scratch deep grooves, run away, poop/pee in house, aggressive or beta

Cats: Feral or Tame: Bite, scratch deep grooves, run away, poop/pee in house, aggressive or beta

Bunnies: They kick, scratch and bite when hopping mad. It takes a lot to get them that way though.

Birds: Large, small, talking

Fish: Fresh or Salt water

Reptiles: Snakes, Iguanas

Cows: These guys will generally leave you alone. Bulls will not.

Goats: Easy to maintain. They will eat anything.

Let's start by discussing potty training. Recently I've been helping train a 6 month old rescue/bought from store. Owner uses puppy potty pads unscented. I recommend Nature's Miracle products because they are all natural, eat the pheromones and enzymes leaving house and furniture smelling like furniture and not an outhouse. These products don't harm the pets or the humans. Right now we are using bleach cleaner.

Kennel training vs Potty pads vs. notice pick up and deposit outside while going to train:

I have used 2 out of three. When puppies are born I begin training when they start walking. See them start to pee or poop? Pick them up and immediately place outside where you want them to go. Repeat often.

Kennel training is when you place dog inside for sleeping then take outside immediately you open in morning. Some people leave dogs in kennels all day long. Not me. When potty training, they sleep in there at night and in morning go outside. Then bring back inside and watch carefully until you're sure there will be no accidents.

Potty pads is where you place them on floor you want dog to go on then slowly reduce area size covered and move closer to door until dog is going outside only. Some puppy pads are scented with pheromones to encourage dogs to only go on that pad.

Training is key no matter the animals. You get what you put into it. Be knowledgeable about who you hire if not doing it yourself. Make sure they're not being abused or neglected in the name of training. I ask tons of questions from different reputable people, read books, articles to keep on top of all the changes.

It takes a special kind of person to be able to handle feral animals correctly. Then socialize them into pets. I am one of those people. It is quite often painful in the beginning as no matter your care you will be bitten, clawed up, chase animal around and around until cornered. It usually takes a team of 3 or more people to care for 1 animal when trying to get it in the travel kennel for a vet visit or for applying flea medicine or for giving a bath,

First experiences color the pet's view for life. So handle with care!

Confidentiality of Businesses You Interact With

I am going to talk about what I know, how I did it, tips you can use. You can ask me questions, submit comments or suggestions. It's all about educating others so they don't make the same mistakes I did. We are all going to make them regardless. My mistakes cost me money and inventory. Every time you start a business you are building your reputation. Every person you interact with will either hinder you or help you.

My goal is to help others. This forum helps us reach others outside our network which in the end helps us out.

What I won't do is name names of other businesses or people that I have contracts with now or in the past. Unless that person/company specifically requests it.

Budgeting: Getting It Right the First Time

I actually had help from an existing company putting my budget together. I have a very detailed Excel Formatted Budget that goes from Startup Costs, to monthly recurring costs, to annual recurring costs. I then asked around the different states various ranch owners the costs of running their ranches. They were very open.

Now Budgets for Government Contracts are a whole different sort of numbers. Think in the millions and paid out quarterly with audits to continue with your contract or set aside.

Then there are the Budgets for Grant Applications for your 501c3 nonprofit.

I have them all. I have included them just so you see the huge difference it makes.

Expense Type	Amount	Repeat Payment?	Notes		Income Type	Amount	Repeat Payment?	Notes
credit card terminal & site	$15.00	Monthly			CFC	$9,451.52	See Notes	April: 190.91, July: 3086.87, October: 3086.87, March 2015: 3086.87
Homes for Heroes vids	$1,000.00	Daily			CFC AI	$209.86	No	
office space rental (TN)	$120.00	Monthly			Paypal Donations	$25.00	Montly	
kentucky alliance domain	$10.00	No			Donation tables	$1,500.00	See Notes	June-August; 500 each
trademark Press	$2,466.68	No			Coffee cup sales	$5,000.00	No	
credit card payment	$3,000.00	No			Wildcat's Sanctuary & Ranch donation	$3,500.00	See Notes	Payment depends on Wildcat income
Lighthouse PSA	$5,200.00	No			(Wildcat) Stock	$0.00	See Notes	$250 each, 5000 available
corp. vehicle	$2,000.00	No	donated; one is also in need of repairs		TTWC	$2,500.00	See Notes	December; also donates pet supplies
home repair projects	$100,000.00	No	8A Certification needed		Cavallo Equestrian Arts	$5,000.00	See Notes	3 shows, expenses/income not set yet
purchase ranch (TN)	$50,000.00	No			Grants	$10,000.00	See Notes	200 submitted, money granted TBA
purchase ranch (KY)	$100,000.00	No			Benefactor Annual Donations	$600.00		
pet supplies	$20,000.00	Yearly			Adoption Fees	$500.00	see Notes	Ea dog adoption fee is $250
property taxes	$5,000.00	Yearly			T-Shirt sales	$1,000.00		
gen liability insurance/D&O ins	$2,000.00	No			Paracord Sales	$220.00		
legal Counsel Retainer	$1,000.00	No					grant responses	September 16, 2014. The Summerlee Foundation $5000
car insurance	$126.89	Monthly	car not running, ins not paid til it does					Shumaker Foundation declined
bath certification	$800.00	No	Per person					Patterson foundation declined
first aid certification	$65.00	No	Per person					Quail Roost Foundation, no funding yet. Keep us in mind.
health/dental/vision insurance	$18,176.40	Yearly	For 4 people, $1514.70/mo					Emily Vernon Foundation Followed up 4/23/14
Marketing	$300.00	Monthly						NAVS asked us to reapply using different terminology.
Travel	$1,000.00	No						Binky Foundation Declined
car repairs	$550.00	No	engine scrapped, deal on new one					Scaife Family Foundation declined
laptop	$100.00	See notes	$98 per month, $700 total					Maddie Fund declined
File Retrieval from Hard Drive	$0.00	No	Synergistics, Vet own, Orlando area.					
video conference software	$50.00	Monthly	see Jack for best options					
salaries	$100,000.00	No	when Veteran Rescue can afford performance bas					
Bank Fees	$200.00	No						
past due corp bills	$6,500.00	No						
Duns & Bradstreet	$500.00	See notes	Price per company. $500 estimate based on sale					
office supplies	$1,500.00		8A Certification needed					
Melissa legal	$700.00		Paid off before November					
Financial Mgmt	$1,500.00	Yearly	only when we have over $25000 invest					
Total Expenses	$423,879.97				Total Income	$39,506.38		
							CFC Reponses	Central Fl approved
					Net Income	-$384,373.59		Atlantic Coast denied
								Ft Campbell
								TN/KY
								Suncoast
								NE Fl/SE GA approved

EXPENSE CATEGORY

Expense Category	Expenses. Variabla Monthly	Expenses. Variabla Annual	Expenses· Fixed Monthly	Expenses· Fixed Annual	Start Up Costs
Gas Utilities	$ 200.00	$ 2,400.00			
Electric	$ 1,000.00	$ 12,000.00			
Mortgage			$ 1,250.00	$ 15,000.00	
Phone			S 100.00	S 1,200.00	
Cable			$ 100.00	$ 1,200.00	
Internet			$ 100.00	$ 1,200.00	
Entertainment Food	$ 1,250.00	$ 15,000_00			
Marketing/Advertising	$ 1,750.00	$ 21,000.00			
Funding Manager			S 12.000.00	$ 144,000.00	
Cleaning Supplies	$ 250.00	$ 3,000.00			
Vitamins	$ 150.00	$ 1,300.00			
Purchase land					$ 150,000.00
Construct buildings					$ 150,000.00
Repair Premises					$ 50,000.00
Fence in land					$ 25,000.00
Purchase Equipment					$ 200,000.00
Purchase Electronics					$ 50,000.00
Purchase Office Supplies					$ 10,000.00
Gas for company vehicles	$ 400.00	$ 4,800.00			
Purchase Horses					$ 5,000.00
Purchase Dogs					$ 5,000.00
Purchase other animals					$ 5,000.00
Pet supplies, horse feed/hay	$ 2,500.00	$ 30,000.00			
Purchase company vehicles					$ 30,000.00
Veterinarian Services	$ 2,500.00	$ 30,000.00			
Medical	$ 2,500.00	$ 30,000.00			
Insurances				$ 10,000.00	
Property Taxes			$ 208.33	$ 2,500.00	
Travel Fees					
Payroll Salaries			S 5,000.00	$ 60,000.00	
Blacksmith/Farrier	$ 2,500.00	$ 30,000.00			
	S 15,000.00	S 179,500.00	$ 18,758.33	$ 235,100.00	$ 680,000.00

V· Annual Expense figures ere an
estimate and are sub~cttoc:hange
· Finanda'

data
~pfe$ents.
a SO Acre
horse farm
wlth 2S
working
employees
and 6
horses

Expenses / Annual Variable

Expenses	Annual Variable
Gas Utilities	$ 2,400.00
Electric	12,000.00
Mortgage	$
Phone	
Cable	
Internet	
Entertainment Food	
Marketing/Advertising	15,000.00
Funding Manager	$ 21,000.00
Cleaning Supplies	$
Vitamins	3,000.00
Purchase land	1,300.00
Construct buildings	S
Repair Premises	$
Fence in land	
Purchase Equipment	
Purchase Electronics	
Purchase Office Supplies	
Gas for company vehicles	
Purchase Horses	4,800.00
Purchase Dogs	
Purchase other animals	$
Pet supplies, horse feed/hay	
Purchase company vehicles	30,000.00
Veterinarian Services	
Medical	
Insurances	30,000.00
Property Taxes	$ 30,000.00
Travel Fees	
Payroll Salaries	
Blacksmith/Farrier	$
	$ 30,000.00
	$
	$ 179,500.00

Variable E:xp'ense./Annual)

Gas Utllltl | Electric

Blacksmith/Farrier   001.   ~tertatnment

17 ...._'_   7 ~   Food

●

P~6Jies
010

Medl,"1
17

Services

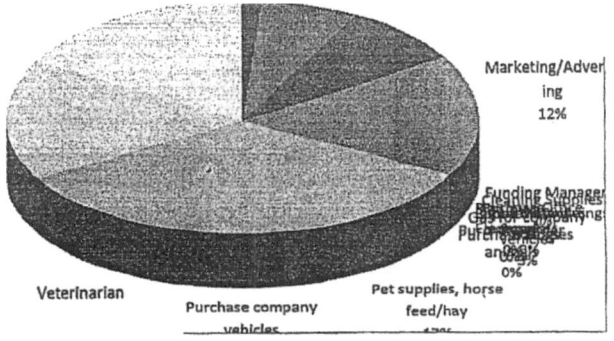

Expenses / Annual Fixed

L ____

Expenses	Annual Fixed
Gas Utilities	
Electric	
Mortgage	S 15,000.00
Phone	
Cable	$ 1,200.0
Internet	S 0
Entertainment Food	S 1,200.0
Marketing/Advertising	0
Funding Manager	1,200.00
Cleaning Supplies	S
Vitamins	
Purchase land	144.000.00
Construct buildings	
Repair Premises	
Fence in Land	
Purchase Equipment	
Purchase Electronics	
Purchase Office Supplies	
Gas for company vehicles	
Purchase Horses	
Purchase Dogs	
Purchase other animals	
Pet supplles, horse feed/hay	
Purchase company vehicles	
Veterinarian Services	
Medical	
Insurances	
Property Taxes	
Travel Fees	
Payroll Salaries	$ 10,000.00
Blacksmith/Farrier	
	$ 2,500.00
	$ 60,000.00

•

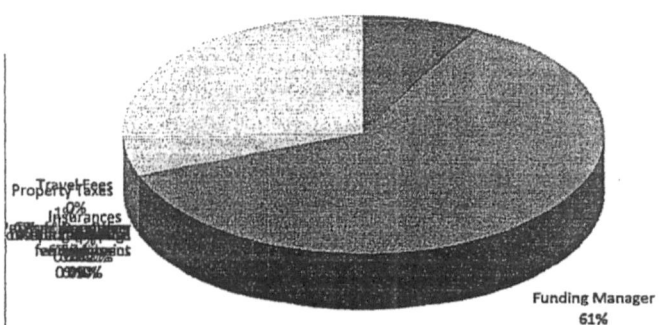

Payroll Salaries $ 235,100.00

26

Fixed EXDPns P IAnnua~lng;/Allllertis
m.~ rtg.gep~

     0   6   ~ow!

Expenses	Startup
Gas Utilities	
Electric	
Mortgage	
Phone	
Cable	
Internet	
Entertainment Food	
Marketing/Advertising	
Funding Manager	
CleanIng Supplies	
Vitamins	
Purchase land	$ 150,000.00
Construct buildings	$ 150,000.00
Repair Premises	$ 50,000.00
Fence in land	$ 25,000.00
Purchase Equipment	$ 200,000.00
Purchase Electronics	$ 50,000.00
Purchase Office Supplies	S 10,000.00
Gas for company vehicles	
Purchase Horses	$ 5,000.00
Purchase Dogs	$ 5,000.00
Purchase other animals	$ 5,000.00
Pet supplies, horse feed/hay	
Purchase company vehicles	$ 30,000.00
Veterinarian Services	
Medical	
Insurances	
Property Taxes	
Travel Fees	
Payroll Salaries	
Blacksmith/Farrier	
	$ 680,000.00

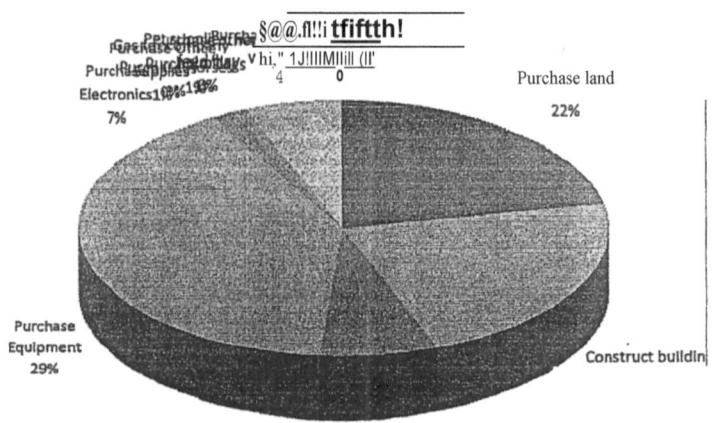

VA's Supportive Services for Veteran Families Program
Exhibit III: Applicant Budget - Quarterly SSVF Grant Funds Budget

*Please note that the SSVF application instructions for Exhibit III refer to monthly expenditure projections. Applicants need only project quarterly expenditures in this submission.

Name of Applicant:	Animal Rescue & Veteran Support Services, Corp.
	DBA Veteran Rescue
SSVF Grant Amount:	$1,000,000.00
Application Fiscal Year:	FY 2013

Program Expenses	# FTE	% FTE	Base Annual Salary/Wage	% of Total SSVF Grant	SSVF Grant Funds Total Annual	SSVF Grant Funds Quarter 1	SSVF Grant Funds Quarter 2	SSVF Grant Quarte
I. Provision and Coordination of Supportive Services (Minimum of 90% of Total SSVF Grant Amount)								
1. Personnel/Labor Title and Organization								
President Veteran Rescue			50,000.00	6%	$ 56,349.00	$ 15,000.00	$ 13,000.00	$
Executive Assistant Veteran Rescue				3%	$ 28,000.00	$ 7,000.00	$ 7,000.00	$
Foreman Veteran Rescue				3%	$ 28,000.00	$ 7,000.00	$ 7,000.00	$
Ranch Hands Veteran Rescue				3%	$ 28,000.00	$ 7,000.00	$ 7,000.00	$
Rehabilatative Therapists Veteran Rescue				15%	$ 150,000.00	$ 45,000.00	$ 30,000.00	$
Interns Veteran Rescue				2%	$ 23,000.00	$ 8,000.00	$ 5,000.00	$
Medical Staff Veteran Rescue				20%	$ 200,000.00	$ 50,000.00	$ 50,000.00	$
Cleaning Staff Veteran Rescue				5%	$ 45,000.00	$ 20,000.00	$ 10,000.00	$
				0%	$ -	$ -	$ -	$
				0%	$ -	$ -	$ -	$
				0%	$ -	$ -	$ -	$
				0%	$ -	$ -	$ -	$
				0%	$ -	$ -	$ -	$
				0%	$ -	$ -	$ -	$
				0%	$ -	$ -	$ -	$
				0%	$ -	$ -	$ -	$
				0%	$ -	$ -	$ -	$
				0%	$ -	$ -	$ -	$
Subtotal Salaries/Wages				56%	$ 558,349.00	$ 159,000.00	$ 129,000.00	$
Fringe Benefits @				0%	$ -	$ -	$ -	$
Subtotal Personnel				56%	$ 558,349.00	$ 159,000.00	$ 129,000.00	$
2. Temporary Financial Assistance				0.00%	$ -			
3. Other Non-Personnel Provision and Coordination of Supportive Services Expenses								
Required VA Training (mandatory)				0%	$ 3,000.00	$ -	$ -	$
Path EAP Training				0%	$ 2,000.00	$ 2,000.00		
Purchase of Facilities				30%	$ 300,000.00	$ 100,000.00	$ 50,000.00	$
Theraputic Jacuzzi				1%	$ 10,000.00	$ 5,000.00	$ 5,000.00	
Supplies				2%	$ 20,100.00	$ 8,100.00	$ 5,000.00	$
				0%	$ -	$ -	$ -	$
				0%	$ -	$ -	$ -	$
				0%	$ -	$ -	$ -	$
				0%	$ -	$ -	$ -	$
				0%	$ -	$ -	$ -	$
				0%	$ -	$ -	$ -	$
				0%	$ -	$ -	$ -	$
				0%	$ -	$ -	$ -	$
				0%	$ -	$ -	$ -	$
				0%	$ -	$ -	$ -	$
				0%	$ -	$ -	$ -	$
Subtotal Other Program Expenses				34%	$ 335,100.00	$ 115,100.00	$ 60,000.00	$
4. Lease & Maintenance of Vehicle(s)			# of Vehicles 1	2%	$ 16,000.00	$ 4,000.00	$ 4,000.00	$
Subtotal Provision and Coordination of Supportive Services				90.94%	909,449.00	278,100.00	193,000.00	
II. Administrative Expenses (Maximum of 10% of Total SSVF Grant Amount)								
General Liability Insurance				0%	$ 570.00	$ -	$ -	$
Directors and Officers Insurance				0%	$ 634.00	$ 634.00	$ -	$
Health Insurance				1%	$ 6,000.00	$ 1,500.00	$ 1,500.00	$
Rehabilatative Obstacle Courses				8%	$ 75,000.00	$ 25,000.00	$ 20,000.00	$
Travel Expenses				0%	$ 1,500.00	$ 500.00	$ 500.00	$
Utilities				0%	$ 2,847.00	$ 949.00	$ 949.00	$
Office Equipment				0%	$ 4,000.00	$ 1,000.00	$ 1,000.00	$
				0%	$ -	$ -	$ -	$
				0%	$ -	$ -	$ -	$
				0%	$ -	$ -	$ -	$
				0%	$ -	$ -	$ -	$
				0%	$ -	$ -	$ -	$
				0%	$ -	$ -	$ -	$
				0%	$ -	$ -	$ -	$
				0%	$ -	$ -	$ -	$
				0%	$ -	$ -	$ -	$
Subtotal Administrative Expenses				9.06%	$ 90,551.00	$ 29,583.00	$ 23,949.00	$ 1
Grand Total				100.00%	$ 1,000,000.00	$ 307,683.00	$ 216,949.00	$ 273
% of Total SSVF Grant					100.0%	30.8%	21.7%	

Where To Go For Funding

Angel Investors, Venture capitalists, Bank, Friends and Family, Sale of Stock, Donations, Contracts, etc. Let's take each of these one at a time to see what might be right for you.

First off your personal credit score has a lot to do with how your approval or denial comes about. Your Business Plan is next to get dissected. Marketing Plan and your personal enthusiasm as you present your 60 second elevator speech also make an impact.

Be careful where you find these sources, as there are a ton of scammers out there including on LinkedIn.

Angels: I can vouch for 3 out of 100's I've approached. Do your homework. Find a reputable agency or person who can vouch for one.

Venture Capital: Again I met 100's through LinkedIn and Google Searches. Only 1 was legit.

Bank: Must have a very high personal credit score, 10% of funds you are asking for minimum, and equity in home too. That will get you a maybe. Some banks restrict where you can apply for a mortgage or a line of credit. Bank loans too vary. I've dealt with at least 6 different banks both local and national.

Friends and Family: Unless they are a millionaire with money to burn, don't ask. Unless you like being lonely and shunned, don't ask.

Stock: Corporations can have shares of stock issued can can sell personally to known associates and family to avoid any SEC rulings and fines. Small and startups go this route. But stock is worthless practically speaking until after 3 years in business making a profit.

Donations: Non For Profits go this route. This includes the CFC Program (Combined Federal Contribution). 100% Tax Deductible. This is how 99% of non profits operate and survive from year to year.

Contracts: Levy Restaurants will contract with your nonprofit organization to donate to your cause. You work for your money.

We started out doing this until there was a management change which altered the rules of size of organizations that could work.

Government Contracts are the biggie every for profit wants: Millions of dollars per year. The process for this is long, time consuming, and then you bid, and then you also have to be on the GSA Schedule or Categories to get noticed. Don't bother paying the companies that call you up unless you have money to burn. Find someone already working on contract and get their help if possible. Otherwise if left with no choice pay $300/year.

Thinking Outside The Box

How many of you entrepreneurs think outside the box when it comes to getting clients or raising funds? I learned that after 3 years of networking my companies I had to do something different if I wanted my companies to thrive.

So for my nonprofit since traditional fundraising methods didn't work for my situation, it was time for outside the box solutions. Golf tournaments are nice and all but if you can't get more than 16 people to sign up in 9 months it's time to go elsewhere. Which I did.

Alas the same goes for a for profit company. So since banks, investors, friends, and family are all out the door for solutions to generating start up capitol, I have moved onto ...wait for it...writing a book and self-publishing to bring in revenue. Having worked as an Assistant Manager and Bookseller in the book world I know the ins/outs there pretty well. Barnes and Noble in my opinion is struggling, Borders which owned Waldenbooks went under, actually I think Barnes and Nobles bought them out too. Wholesale discount bargain books went under. Amazon and Kindle and small bookstores are pretty much where you go to sell. Plus by using Smile.Amazon.com to purchase (Amazon's donation site exact same as Amazon.com) you're helping your nonprofit generate donations by purchasing.

Using my knowledge, and my style of writing and knowing where to go to get things done means anyone can do this. I mean there are literally hundreds of business books most of which I found wordy and of no help at all. And we're talking big names in the business world.

By writing a business book that is short and to the point, it is immediately useful to all, and by self-publishing it is immediately available to all for sale on Amazon or Kindle.

I do a lot of networking and collaborating to help others. I don't charge for this as people say I should. I collaborate with other small startup nonprofits mostly because they need the help and I've already been there.

If you have a non for profit that is a 501c3 approved, then you can also speak to executives at local airports asking if they will donate space so your organization can sell your products to everyone passing through. In my case coffee cups or   T-Shirts or Paracord Items, etc. You get the idea.

Donation Table Events outside your local stores. You contact Store Manager for assistance in getting on their calendar.

Standing in the Medians at Stop lights with a donation container. You see the City Tax Collector Office for that one.

So when you decide you want to start a business, no matter the type, start thinking and planning years in advance for budgeting matters. If traditional fundraising doesn't work for you, or you just bootstrap it, go to thinking outside the box. In the business world it does not matter if what you try comes from an era bygone, if it works go with it. Don't just try one avenue, try them all until you find what works, then tweak it as needed.

#Christihubbard #business #book #fundraise #forprofit #nonprofit

Honesty, Integrity, Ethics, Accountability

You make or break your business reputation with each contact you make. With each program you offer, with each person you help. You must have honor, integrity, and ethics or you will be shut down by the IRS or State Officials if you put a foot wrong. Ever wonder why your business has slowed to nothing? Why all your emails come back as spam? Let's think about how long you have been in business. Is your reputation torn to shreds over perceived slights?

Make sure the timeline you give for any event or project is realistic. Always communicate to the other party involved if anything changes. Minimum time for any fundraising is 6 weeks for raffles and auctions to 9 Months for golf tournaments and black tie dinners.

Accountability. Is it just for audits?

What does accountability mean to you? To your business? Is it just for audits? I sure hope not.

As you know I have 3 different types of companies and I have controls for all three that works for me. It ensures I have accountability at all times and cruise through any audits that come up for various reasons.

When applying for grants, when applying for CFC, when the IRS asks for information, when a potential donor requests to see documentation, when asking for a bank loan, a line of credit, etc. You get the idea.

I love it when funds are "guaranteed" only to arrive late or not at all. Just how many excuses can one person come up with to excuse this? Do you think your vendors or clients care about them? The answer is NO. It really is a balancing act when dealing with vendors, clients, and other organizations.

If someone on your Advisory board tells you point blank not to collect documentation of any kind, it's time to set them straight or ask them to leave. If they say one thing and then do another, it's time to go. That's a version of fraud when it comes to funds for your charity. They ask you to add a program that falls within your Mission and then turns out to be a "slush fund" that you were not informed of, it's time to hold a meeting to let everyone know what's going on. The fact the perpetrator is a Veteran owned business that partnered with you is just one reason why they're getting such a bad reputation.

Another situation that came up was a Veteran with PTSD/TBI/Drugged out of his mind had memory issues. He started appointing people to my board with no authority. He then wanted 100% of funds that came into the Program he was in charge of for himself, not the program. The Board voted him off after he was apprised of the laws he was breaking and fraud he was perpetrating.

A Veteran wanted to partner with Veteran Rescue on a handshake deal, no legal documents signed of any kind. Again he had PTSD/Medication. Did not happen.

PTSD was just one of the things they had in common. I'm pretty sure they all lacked jobs, or were really tight for funding. I tried to find Board Members who had skills I lacked. I have multiple programs that help Veteran and animals nationwide. I focus on Florida for the animals, and do what I can for the rest.

People will try to take advantage of you especially if you're a woman owned company. **You need people who support you not take you for every penny they can.** If anything they should respect my organization's transparency and commitment to have an above board and top running operation.

Sample of Recent Not For Profit Board Meeting issues: We will be going over these documents at the meeting. Please familiarize yourself with them. If you have questions I will gladly answer them.

Some of these documents such as donor sources are confidential and not to be distributed to the general public.

If a Board Member leaves the Board and uses this information in a harmful way, I will sue on behalf of the organization.

I do have Non disclosure forms to be signed and returned. I believe maybe we should be enforcing that rule for our Board.

My organization is an open book. Receipts are on file, client files are confidential, my 990 is in full public view on website, Charity Navigator and more.

To question my honesty and integrity and then say you didn't mean to offend but then to say don't make me your enemy I will sabotage you publicly is an offense.

You can see I have been helping others including Veterans as much as I possibly can given financial resources we have. It has not been 2 years between helping Veterans.

Yes Veteran Rescue has accumulated expenses that do need to be paid.

Yes it is legal to use your personal vehicle for business purposes and write off the repairs, mileage, gas, and more.

The organization is healthier than ever this year.

Yes it is legal to ask for documentation such as DD214, medical diagnosis, military ID, estimates from contractors and more including photos of before and after repairs for clients requesting assistance. Every non profit, government agency, VA, etc asks for it before treating. It is required for audits among other reasons. It is kept confidential. Not one of my clients have complained.

This keeps are budget reasonable and our clients legit. We do not have bottomless pockets to help every person who says I tell the truth. We have learned our lessons there over the years.

Sample of Recent Board Agenda including event calendar dates: Current budget numbers updated, see attached Excel.

Fundraisers: CFC, TTWC, Donation Table, Removed for privacy Raffle, Auction, coffee cups. What did we learn, Are there any changes we should implement?

Bills: Past due all paid off but 2:

Moving Forward. Purchasing Ranch, Travel, Marketing, Video, Programs

This will be the first year we will have a surplus of funds. They must be utilized wisely in case of emergencies.

Refresher on Veteran Rescue for our board Members in other States who will be representing us and speaking with CFC employees. VA Hospitals, Post Offices, Military Bases, etc.

Who we are, what we do, how we help, why we help. Documentation we collect on clients and why we do, Documentation we need for audits.

Sample of Recent Results of this kind of meeting: New meeting features: Skype call recorder! This is to help Melissa dictate notes, or for anything we may have to refer back to at a later date, etc. *If you have a problem with being recorded, please let us know before the meeting!*

Voting:
1. Add a program (Sponsor MMA Training for Veterans with PTSD with proper documentation) if yes TN only or Nationwide? Cap of how many a year?
Against having no documentation [everyone except one]
Add a program [no]

Note: Documentation is needed for Veteran Rescue's protection in an audit. Per Removed for privacy – there is a stigma with documentation, insults PTSD Veterans and are looking forward to more of a "handshake" deal

2. Change how we do fundraisers, types of fundraisers, length of time we hold one, who we allow to host on our behalf, etc.
6 weeks minimum timeframe is **required** in order to host a fundraiser for Veteran Rescue. All funds agreed upon *up front* must remain and cannot be changed without mutual agreement by both parties.

Anyone in possession of Veteran Rescue, signage, banners, products, etc, must pay up front costs associated with them so Veteran Rescue programs can continue without interruption.
Removed for privacy: $750

3. Cap or tweak our current programs. If yes, what do we do about our waiting list?
Removed for privacy - Limited amount of services, don't spread yourself too thin. Can be fluid, based on donations

Voted to keep current programs on website. Home repair project is being capped and may not be continued after finishing the current waiting list

4. Prune our Board Members down as recommended? Change how we pick them, where we pick them from, serve with no voting rights for a specific term until voted in or out?
Pruning: Removed for privacy – yes [7]. We appreciate your service and abilities on our behalf, including the fundraising raffle. We wish you the best of luck in your future endeavors. Your support is more than welcome in any future events.

Future Board Members will be added by a vote after serving several months as an intern to see if they are a good fit. **Non-disclosure Document signed up front.**

5. Partnerships/Collaborations with other entities: Yes/No/With limits (what documentation would we require)
Within limits – the board must vote and **documentation and a non-disclosure agreement is required** up front.

Veteran organization provided collaboration document written by an attorney, was passed by the board as sufficient MMA gym documentation is required for a collaboration, however the sponsor a veteran with PTSD for MMA training will not be a part of the programs we offer.

Thank you all for going out of your way to assist us.

1 Change in our CFC Speaking Events. We changed New Port Richey to Tampa. That date will be made available next week.

Veteran Rescue is participating in several CFC Events where we have a table and we speak to others. August Events. Others will be added as they are offered.

July 6 Board Meeting 1PM, EST: 1 grant being decided on this summer

July 19 Auction Ends

July 19 and 20 we will again be out front Publix, (Rinehart and Timacuan) in Lake Mary.

Board Meeting Aug 3rd, 1PM EST

August 20th – Lakeland, 8:30 – 11:30am, Lakeland Main Post Office, 2800 Lakeland Hills Blvd., Lakeland, FL 33810

Aug 23 and 24 we will again be out front Publix, (Rinehart and Timacuan) in Lake Mary.

August 28th - Tampa, 8:30am - 1pm

Aug 23rd and Aug 24th we will again be out front Publix, (Rinehart and Timacuan) in Lake Mary.

Sept 7, 1PM EST Board Meeting: 1 grant being decided on for Veteran Rescue

Sept 20 CFC Event Night with the Rays

Oct 5th Board Meeting, 1PM EST

Oct 13 CFC Golf Tournament

Oct 26, 1-4PM Temple Terrace Womans Club Fundraiser, FL

Nov 2nd, Board Meeting 1PM EST: 2 grants being decided on for Veteran Rescue

Dec 7th, 1PM EST Board Meeting

*********UNIVERSAL GIVING APPROVED BEGINNING THIS YEAR, ANYONE WHO HAS OUR CFC #19270, CAN GIVE MONEY TO US REGARDLESS OF LOCATION!!**************

Winning Awards and Marketing

I have to date 6 awards for the last 4 years for 2 of my companies combined. This has brought me business to my door when I published that information on my websites, and on all forms of social media. I have videos, photos, and dozens of referrals I put on my website from others who have sent me the referral.

My Marketing plan actually came to me as a gift from Nova University School of business Students of Professor Dena Hale. I can't thank her enough.

I have 2 different types of business plans. 1 is 8 pages, KISS Method, and the bank loved it. The other has the Marketing Plan for Nova University in it and the banks raved as did the investors. This business plan is over 30 pages long. It has the same Outline as the first but is not using KISS Method.

I don't know the first thing about Marketing, so I utilize my family that excel in I.T. My webmaster is WordPress Happy which uses plugins that do the bulk of my marketing for me and it's free.

PSA's or Public Service Announcements. When any nonprofit are offered these, go for them! They are free to the organization and bring in tons of new supporters and donations. Once you have a PSA in hand upload that video to all your websites, all your social media sites, upload to YouTube, and pop into emails to friends and family to share.

Websites: Do It Yourself and Look Great

WordPress is my friend and yours. Easy to use, free, and deals with the ugly side of Marketing and SEO Optimization, etc. Your Website looks and feels professional, and I can update it myself without needing a computer tech's help.

There is absolutely no need to pay thousands of dollars for this service. Believe me unless you have money to burn, just ignore all those sales emails and phone calls.

Domains:

Who needs to pay $30 when $5 or $9 will do? I purchased my domains through cheap domain and some were on sale through Web or Register. Both of those sites though will scam you for thousands of dollars and as such I don't use them for anything other than my on sale domain name.

BlueHost is who I have my paid web hosting through. Easy to use, very helpful when you call, and did not cost me an arm and a leg. I am able to have all my businesses hosted for free on this server and all my other business domains are also hosted for free plus unlimited emails, etc.

As of this writing I have 20 domains on my server with multiple emails for each one and all of it looks professional.

If you want to go professional instead of do it yourself I recommend Computer Tech's Castle. http://computertechscastle.com/ Affordable, reliable, quick service by qualified personnel.

Social Media Is your Friend

LinkedIn, Facebook, Twitter, and YouTube just to name a few of the big ones you will want to create accounts for. It is important that each business, each personal account be kept separate. For instance I have 3 businesses and a personal account with each. I also of separate groups for my businesses on LinkedIn.

This is a great way to build your brand and your reputation. By posting every day at least 3 times a day at different hours you will see an increase in traffic to your website and office.

LinkedIn is where I receive 90% of my business referrals and supporters worldwide. It is also how I contacted local radio stations, newspapers, celebrities, and business owners we could utilize resources from.

Local radio stations and online radio such as Readers Entertainment and Chairborne Commandos and SOFREP are all good sources of online radio publicity spots for not for profits. This in turn drives website traffic and donations as well as offers for volunteering, other agencies or organizations looking to do a community project, etc.

Some radio stations are owned by one big corporation and will typically repeat or re-air your interview without it looking like a repeat interview at different times or month or quarter. For instance Clear Channel Radio owns over 80 stations nationwide so my one interview went nationwide multiple times.

Moving on to your local newspapers, reporters, and TV anchors. Then when you have sufficient notice go national TV anchors, reporters, and TV Stations airing PSA or interviewing your organization.

Each of these events drives web traffic, volunteer offers, and donations of money or in kind.

Make short 1 or 2 minute videos of each project or program. Get client referrals or thank you's and add them to all your sites. Take lots of pictures. Get legal and liability release forms signed so you can use the photos and videos of clients and others you've helped.

THE END